Regions of the United States: The Southwest

Mark Stewart

Raintree

Chicago, Illinois

© 2006 Raintree
an imprint of Capstone Global Library,LLC
Chicago, Illinois

Customer Service 888-363-4266

Visit our website at www.heinemannraintree.com

Produced for Raintree by
White-Thomson Publishing Ltd,
Bridgewater Business Centre,
210 High Street, Lewes, BN7 2NH

For information, address the publisher:
Raintree, 100 N. LaSalle, Suite 1200, Chicago, IL 60602

Page layout by Clare Nicholas
Photo research by Stephen White-Thomson
Illustrations by John Fleck
Printed and bound in China by CTPS

15 14 13 12 11
10 9 8 7 6 5 4 3 2 1

**Library of Congress
Cataloging-in-Publication Data**

Stewart, Mark, 1960-
  The Southwest / Mark Stewart.
    p. cm. -- (Regions of the USA)
  Includes bibliographical references and index.
  ISBN 1-4109-2309-6 (hc) -- ISBN 1-4109-2317-7 (pb)
  1. Southwestern States--Juvenile literature. I. Title. II. Series.
  F786.S877 2007
  979--dc22
                        2006004815

Acknowledgments
The publisher would like to thank the following for permission to reproduce photographs:
p. 4 David Frazier; pp. 4-5, 9A, 14-15, 20-21, 24-25, 28, 31B, 35, 39, 41, 43A, 47, 48, 49, 51 27B, 40, 42, 46 Kerrick James; p. 6 Oklahoma City; p. 8 Jeffrey Greenberg; pp. 9B, 17B, 23 Tom Till; p. 10 Angelico Chavez History Library; pp. 11, 21, 22, 43B Joe Viesti/viestiphoto.com; p. 12 Texas State Library and Archives Commission; p. 13 Friends of the Governor's Mansion; pp. 16, 32 Larry Kolvoord/viestiphoto.com; pp. 17A, 28-29 Maile Rich-Griffith; pp. 18-19, 30, 36, 37 Kevin Vandivier/viestiphoto.com; p. 20 Robert Winslow/viestiphoto.com; p. 22 Kathleen Cook; p. 25 Eric Wessman/viestiphoto.com; p. 26 John Balu/San Diego Scenics; pp. 27A, 44B, 45B Mark Stewart; p. 31A Native Stock.com; p. 33 Richard Cummins/viestiphoto.com; p. 34 Don Mason/CORBIS; p. 38 Greg Smith/CORBIS; pp. 44A, 45A Icon SMI/Corbis; p. 50 Martha Cooper/viestiphoto.com

Cover photo of Grand Canyon reproduced with permission of Kerrick James

Contents

Some words are shown in bold, **like this.** You can find out what they mean by looking in the glossary.

The Southwest

The United States has been called a "melting pot" because of the many races and **cultures** it mixes together. The Southwest region of the country began this American **tradition** when the Europeans and Native Americans first met 500 years ago.

Since that time, the face of the Southwest has changed many times over. However, one thing remains the same. Across the states of Arizona, New Mexico, Texas, and Oklahoma, the people who live there continue to blend their lives and cultures in new and interesting ways.

These children are enjoying the festivities at the Texas State Fair.

Hot landscapes

The Southwest owes its beauty to the forces of nature, which have shaped the region for millions of years. Some of its most amazing landscapes are in Arizona, where one volcano was active less than 1,000 years ago. It formed Sunset Crater, which can be seen today at Sunset Crater Volcano National Monument near Flagstaff, Arizona.

Cultural blend

The spirit of the Southwest shows the blending of cultures at every turn, from its people and history to its food and **pastimes** to its cities and towns. Even the weather, animals, and plants of the Southwest reflect a blending—of hot and cold, big and small, and common and uncommon.

This book explores a vast region of the country. It includes **deserts**, mountains, noisy cities, and small, quiet towns. Some of the wildest places on Earth can be found in the Southwest. Often they are just a short distance from the most civilized.

All roads lead to adventure in the Southwest. Arizona's spectacular Monument Valley is just ahead.

Find out later...

Where will you find this amazing cave?

What is a "Buffalo Soldier?"

By which famous road is this car parked?

You are here

The Southwest region is made up of three of the largest states in the country—Arizona, New Mexico, Texas—and Oklahoma. These states cover more than a half-million square miles (1.3 million square kilometers), and are home to more than 33 million people.

Some of the important places you will read about in this book include Phoenix, Tucson, and Sedona in Arizona; Santa Fe, Albuquerque, and Taos in New Mexico; Houston, Austin, Dallas, San Antonio, Fort Worth, Galveston, and El Paso in Texas; and Oklahoma City and Tulsa in Oklahoma.

Just as important are the region's small towns. Like the big cities of the Southwest, each has its own personality and flavor. You will learn about many of these special places in this book, too.

Each of the major cities of the Southwest has its own unique look. The Myriad Botanical Gardens provides an urban oasis for residents of Oklahoma City.
▼

Name that state!

Each state in the Southwest got its name in a different way. Arizona comes from *arizonac*, a Native American word for little spring. New Mexico has had the same name for centuries. Settlers who journeyed north from Mexico called it *Nueva* (new) Mexico to remind them of home. Texas comes from *tejas*, a Native American word for friend. Oklahoma took its name from two Choctaw words—*okla*, meaning people and *humma*, meaning red.

Fact file

State	Population	Size
Arizona	5,743,834	113,635 sq. mi. (294,315 sq. km)
New Mexico	1,903,289	121,356 sq. mi. (314,312 sq. km)
Oklahoma	3,523,553	68,667 sq. mi. (177,848 sq. km)
Texas	22,490,022	261,797 sq. mi. (678,054 sq. km)

People and History

Clovis

In 1932, **archaeologists** found evidence of an early Native American culture in Clovis, New Mexico. The Clovis people were in the Southwest more than 10,000 years ago. Scientists believe they were the first people to settle in the Southwest. These people made finely crafted spear points and were excellent hunters.

From western Arizona to southern Texas, the Southwest shares a border with Mexico. More than one-quarter of the people in the Southwest can trace their family's history to Mexico. For many people, speaking Spanish is as common as speaking English.

There was a time, however, when Spanish was not spoken at all in the Southwest. For thousands of years, **nomadic** hunters roamed the area following big game such as **bison** and elk. About 3,000 years ago, small groups of these people began settling along the Rio Grande. As they learned to farm, communities grew from a few dozen to several thousand people.

Some Native American dwellings, such as these in Arizona, were built right into the sides of cliffs. ▶

Pueblos

The small cities that formed along the Rio Grande were called **pueblos.** Around AD 700 to 900, the Pueblo people began to build walls for protection from their enemies. Sometimes, pueblos were built into the sides of cliffs. The people who lived in the Southwest during this time felt a deep connection to the land.

These societies broke apart when changes to the **climate** such as long droughts made it difficult to grow food. Some of these Pueblo people joined the Hopi people of Arizona. Others blended in with the Apache and Navajo groups that moved into the region from the north.

The history of the Southwest is preserved at sites like these ruins of an ancient pueblo at Bandalier National Monument.

This young Navajo woman lives in Arizona. Her **ancestors** have lived in the Southwest for many centuries.

The Anasazi

Among the pueblo-building people who once lived in the Southwest region were the Anasazi. Their archaeolgical sites are the most amazing in the Southwest region. Their former pueblos include cliff dwellings at the Bandalier National Monument, located in northern New Mexico.

Cabeza de Vaca

The first white man to spend time among the Native Americans of the Southwest was Alvar Nuñez Cabeza de Vaca. The Arawanka people captured him after he was shipwrecked on Galveston Island in 1528. De Vaca impressed his captors with some basic medical skills and he became a "medicine man." However, what he was really after was gold, which he tried to find in the Southwest after his captors released him, but he never did.

European contact

When European explorers first came to the Southwest, they found farming communities and nomadic cultures that had existed for hundreds of years. The first white people to arrive in the Southwest were from Spain. The Spanish had already conquered lands in South and Central America before arriving here.

The search for gold

A group led by Francisco Vásquez de Coronado explored the Southwest in search of gold during the early 1540s. At the time there was a legend that there were "cities of gold" in what is today Arizona. Coronado found no gold, but he did make important discoveries about the land and its people.

Before Europeans arrived in Texas, the area was home to Apache and other Native American groups.

Spanish settlement

The first European settlement in the Southwest was established in 1598. Juan de Oñate led a group of miners, ranchers, and farmers up the Rio Grande Valley from Mexico. In 1610 Santa Fe, the second-oldest city in the United States, was born.

It took more than a century for the native people of the region to learn to live with their new neighbors. Slowly but surely, the two cultures began to blend together, and a new culture was created that embraced the customs and religions of both groups.

Many Spanish missions, such as Mission San Xavier del Bac in Tucson, Arizona, are still in use today.

Spanish missions

When the Spanish arrived in the Southwest, they built religious centers called missions. Their goal was to convert the local people to Catholicism, which they hoped would help to control them and make them better citizens. The style of these buildings was often a mix between Spanish and Native American designs.

In 1800 Spain gave control of what is now Oklahoma to France. Three years later, France sold this territory to the United States as part of the **Louisiana Purchase.** In the 1830s the U.S. government forced many Native Americans to move to Oklahoma, which it called Indian Territory.

In 1821 Mexico declared independence from Spain. Mexico encouraged settlers and traders to come to its land. That same year a trade route from Missouri to Santa Fe was created. It was called the Santa Fe Trail. In Texas, which was part of Mexico then, white settlers started a colony. It grew into the city of Austin.

The Trail of Tears

During the 1830s, five Native American tribes—the Cherokee, Chickasaw, Choctaw, Creek, and Seminole— were forced by the United States to leave their lands in the Southeast and move to Oklahoma. During the winter of 1838–1839, thousands died on the 1,000-mile (1,600-kilometer) march westward. The route they followed is now called the Trail of Tears.

This painting shows Stephen Austin, who started a colony in Texas ▶ in 1821.

Fact file
New Mexico and Arizona became U.S. territories in 1846, when they were occupied by the U.S. Army during a war with Mexico.

Independent thinkers

As the Mexican citizens living in the Texas region met more American settlers, they began to talk about declaring independence from Mexico. In 1836 Texans rose up against the Mexican government. They fought and lost a great battle against the Mexican Army at the Alamo, in San Antonio. They won their independence later that year and declared themselves a **republic**. For nine years, Texas was its own country! In 1845 the United States made Texas its 28th state.

From the mid-1800s to the early 1900s, the Southwest was a wild place, full of danger. Thousands of Americans streamed into the region each year hoping to start new lives and new businesses. This marked the beginning of the modern era in Arizona, New Mexico, Texas, and Oklahoma.

American hero Davy Crockett fights off Mexican soldiers in a scene from the Battle of the Alamo in February 1836, painted in 1903.

Sooners

In 1889 the U.S. government opened up the land in Oklahoma to settlers hoping for a better life. All the settlers were supposed to start on the border at the same time and then race for a piece of land. But some sneaky settlers started sooner than everyone else and got the best pieces of land. Today, Oklahomans are nicknamed "Sooners."

Land in the Area

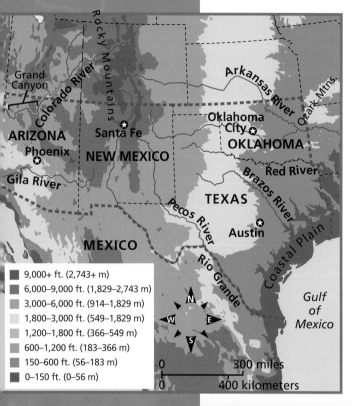

Map Legend (Elevation):
- 9,000+ ft. (2,743+ m)
- 6,000–9,000 ft. (1,829–2,743 m)
- 3,000–6,000 ft. (914–1,829 m)
- 1,800–3,000 ft. (549–1,829 m)
- 1,200–1,800 ft. (366–549 m)
- 600–1,200 ft. (183–366 m)
- 150–600 ft. (56–183 m)
- 0–150 ft. (0–56 m)

0   300 miles
0   400 kilometers

The land and climate of the Southwest differ greatly within the region. From the warm waters of the Gulf of Mexico to the snow-capped mountains of northern New Mexico to the rugged beauty of the Arizona desert, it holds the promise of endless discovery and adventure.

Grand Canyon

Outside its cities much of Arizona is wild desert and forestland. In the north the Colorado River cuts through a high **plateau** to form the Grand **Canyon**. The Grand Canyon is 277 miles (443 kilometers) long and a mile (1.6 kilometers) deep. In some places 21 layers of rock are visible. The oldest rock dates back 1.7 billion years.

The Dust Bowl

In the 1930s much of the farmland in the Southwest dried up and blew away in what became known as the Dust Bowl. Poor farming techniques and years of drought had turned the rich soil to dust. Thousands of farm families left their land and traveled west. Many found work in the fertile valleys of California.

▲ Visitors to the Grand Canyon enjoy the spectacular view from Mather Point.

From the mountains to the gulf

New Mexico marks the southern end of the Rocky Mountains. To the east of the Rockies is the southwestern edge of the Great Plains. Both Texas and New Mexico share a border with Mexico. The land of Texas includes an enormous **coastal plain**, a flat, sandy land located near an ocean or gulf. It can be found along the Gulf of Mexico and is ideal for farming and ranching.

The land of western Oklahoma and northern Texas features **high plains**. Eastern Oklahoma has rolling hills and forests, as well as part of the Ozark Mountains on the border it shares with Missouri and Arkansas. The central part of Oklahoma has wide river valleys.

Fact file

Texas is the second largest state. Alaska, which has 571,951 square miles (1.5 million square kilometers), is more than twice the size of Texas.

High points

The highest point in the Southwest is New Mexico's Wheeler Peak in the *Sangre de Cristo* range, which is part of the Rocky Mountains. It stands at 13,161 feet (4,014 meters). The highest point in Arizona is Humphrey's Peak, at 12,633 feet (3,853 meters). Guadalupe Peak, which rises 8,751 feet (2,669 meters), is the highest point in Texas, while the highest point in Oklahoma is in the Black Mesa area, at 4,973 feet (1,515 meters).

Barton Springs

Barton Springs Pool in Zilker Park in Austin, Texas, is a natural swimming hole. It is fed by an underground spring, which pumps in 32 million gallons (121 million liters) of water each day. The temperature is always 68 °F (20 °C).

The desert

The Southwest may be best known for the Grand Canyon, but the region is full of other incredible sights. Deserts, mountains, **mesas,** and caves especially make the western part of this region a natural wonderland.

Arizona's Painted Desert has amazing pink, purple, and brown-gray rocks, as well as a famous Petrified Forest. The **petrified** wood in the forest was formed more than 200 million years ago. On the Arizona-Utah border, Monument Valley State Park has incredible red earth deserts and rock formations.

Diving into Barton Springs Pool is one way to keep cool in the summer heat of Austin, Texas.

Water

One of the world's largest **aquifers** cuts through central Texas. It provides water to millions of people. The aboveground rivers of the Southwest have been even more crucial to survival in the area. The Rio Grande, Colorado, Brazos, Arkansas, Pecos, and Red Rivers have all played important roles in the region's culture and **economy**.

The biggest body of water in the area is the Gulf of Mexico. It provides food, jobs, entertainment, energy, and transportation to Texas. The state's gulf coastline is 367 miles (590 kilometers) long, stretching from Louisiana to Mexico.

The "Big Room" in Carlsbad Caverns is one of the Southwest region's great natural wonders. ▶

The Rio Grande River winds through New Mexico near Albuquerque. ◀

Wonders underground

One of New Mexico's most amazing natural features is underground, in Carlsbad Caverns National Park. Carlsbad Caverns has three miles (five kilometers) of caves that were formed by an unusual series of geological events. The temperature inside is 56 °F (13 °C) all year, which offers welcome relief from the sizzling summer temperatures at the surface.

Wild weather

The Southwest region has a variety of different climates. Perhaps the most dramatic weather in the United States can be found in Oklahoma. This Southwest state is located in an area where cool, dry winds dip down from the north and warm, humid air moves up from the Gulf of Mexico. This means that there are cold winters and hot summers in Oklahoma.

It also means that Oklahoma has violent thunderstorms, blinding snowstorms, and killer tornados. In fact, central Oklahoma is sometimes called "Tornado Alley." Some of history's deadliest storms have torn through this state.

The awesome beauty of an Oklahoma thunderstorm is best viewed from a few miles away.

▼

Challenging climates

Texas has seen its share of tornados, too. But hurricanes from the Gulf of Mexico are a much greater threat. In 2005 Hurricane Rita smashed into the coast of eastern Texas near Port Arthur, causing flooding and damage to homes and businesses. More than a century earlier, in 1900, a hurricane swept over the island-city of Galveston, killing thousands.

The weather in most parts of New Mexico and Arizona is more predictable than in Texas or Oklahoma. It is also much drier. Summers are very hot and winters are mild. Both states get snow in their mountain areas, but less than two inches of actual rainfall occurs each year in the deserts.

Vicitims of a tornado in Texas survey the damage to their homes. Parts of Texas and Oklahoma are in "Tornado Alley."

Snow birds

Arizona's pleasant winter climate has made it a popular place for people seeking a warm home for the winter. Many people from the Northeast and Midwest fly to the Southwest, where they live for a period of time from November to April. These people are nicknamed "Snow Birds."

Animals and Plants

Big on bats

Bats thrive in the area between San Antonio and Austin, Texas. Most of the bats in this part of Texas are Brazilian or Mexican freetails. The world's largest bat colony is in Bracken Cave, near San Antonio. In Austin people gather each evening to watch the flight of the bats that live under the Congress Avenue Bridge.

The area between the Texas cities of Austin and San Antonio has been called "Bat Heaven."

To the untrained eye, much of the Southwest looks like empty desert. However, dozens of animal species live in this environment. Survival in the desert is a game of hide-and-seek to stay away from predators and out of the fierce sun and heat.

Desert mammals include mule deer, bighorn sheep, jackrabbits, kangaroo rats, ringtail cats, armadillos, cougars, bobcats, and coyotes. Bird species include owls, hawks, turkey vultures, and roadrunners. The desert is also home to tarantulas, scorpions, and a wide variety of reptiles, such as lizards. Lizards of the Southwest include the collared lizard, gecko, and horned lizard, called the horny toad.

Desert snakes

The Southwest has more **species** of rattlesnakes than anywhere else in the world. The sidewinder rattlesnake earns its name by the way it moves across the hot desert sands. The diamondback is easy to identify from its design. Arizona's baseball team is named after this animal.

Other animals

The animals of the Southwest's woodlands and plains include deer, elk, antelope, foxes, opossums, raccoons, beavers, prairie dogs, flying squirrels, and black bears. The American bison was once overhunted but has recently made a comeback.

The armadillo

One of the most beloved animals in the Southwest is the armadillo. Most people believe that armadillos roll into a tight ball when they are threatened, but this is not true. Only one of the many armadillo species can do this. The most common species of armadillo in the Southwest is the nine-banded armadillo.

Great herds of bison once roamed the Southwest. Today they are protected from hunters.

Scientists believe the nine-banded armadillo moved north into the Southwest from South America.

The saguaro

When most people think of the Southwest, they picture deserts dotted with a tall cactus plant with "arms" curving upwards. This cactus is called a saguaro. The saguaro is a master at storing water, and can hold up to 200 gallons (760 liters) at a time. Its waxy coating and sharp spines protect it from animals and extreme temperatures.

The saguaro can live more than 150 years and grow to more than 30 feet (9 meters) tall. It takes a long time for it to get its familiar shape. Its arms do not even begin to form until it is around 75 years old.

A group of tumbleweeds do what they do best—tumble!

Tumbleweeds

Midland, Texas, calls itself the Tumbleweed Capital of the World, even though these plants are not native to the region. These prickly green plants grow all summer, then turn brown and snap off at their stems in the fall. This leaves them free to roll across highways and open fields, spreading their seeds along the way. Some tumbleweeds are over six feet (two meters) tall.

The majestic saguaro cactus is a symbol of the Southwest.

Trees

In the eastern part of the Southwest, the live oak tree provides much-needed shade, as well as a sense of history and pride. Texans and Oklahomans cherish this variety of oak, which has a short, broad trunk and thick, leathery leaves. Many of these have been around for two centuries. Some are named after important people or famous events that took place under them in the mid-1800s. These include the Treaty Oak in Austin, where an important document was signed, and the Sam Houston Oak in Gonzalez, named after one of the early leaders of Texas.

Flower power

The highways of Texas are famous for their sensational wildflowers. This dates back to the 1960s, when First Lady Lady Bird Johnson started a campaign to beautify her home state's major roads. Later, in 1982, Lady Bird Johnson founded the National Wildflower Research Center in Austin, Texas. It was renamed the Lady Bird Johnson Wildflower Center in her honor in 1998.

The rolling hills and river valleys of Oklahoma show bright colors when the leaves begin to change color each autumn.

Cities and Towns

People in the Southwest have always lived near sources of water. The city of Phoenix, Arizona, for example, exists as it does because of the Roosevelt Dam, which was built in 1911 on the Salt River. The dam provides water for drinking and washing and is used for growing food in the surrounding valley.

Rio Grande cities

The city of Santa Fe, New Mexico, was built on top of an existing pueblo located on a **tributary** of the Rio Grande. Down river is the city of Albuquerque, New Mexico's largest city. El Paso, also on the Rio Grande, sits on the Texas border with Mexico, across the river from the Mexican city of Juarez.

Name game

Most towns in the Southwest take their names from Native American or Spanish words, or from important people. Phoenix is different. It is named after the mythical Egyptian bird that rose from a pile of ashes. Phoenix started as a settlement, but died when its canals got clogged up. When the canals were cleaned in 1867, it sprang back to life.

Fact file

Three of America's ten largest cities are in Texas: Houston, Dallas, and San Antonio.

Water and air conditioning helped the city of Phoenix grow to nearly three million people.

Rivers and canals

In Texas, the city of San Antonio honors its water source through its Riverwalk, a 2.5-mile (4-kilometer) waterfront walkway along the San Antonio River.

Houston depends on a body of water called the Ship Channel. This 50-mile (80-kilometer) inlet from the Gulf of Mexico was created after a hurricane wiped out the area's major port, Galveston, in 1900. The channel turned Houston into America's second largest port.

Tulsa, Oklahoma, uses yet another body of water to ship the oil produced there. It travels through the McClellan-Kerr Arkansas River Navigation System, which leads to the Mississippi River and the Gulf of Mexico.

A family enjoys a canoe trip on the Colorado River in the capital city of Austin, Texas.

Town Lake

Another Texas city linked to an important source of water is Austin, the capital of Texas. The city sits along a stretch of the Colorado River in Texas. There are three artificial lakes in the city: Town Lake, Lake Austin, and Lake Walter E. Long. Part of another lake, Lake Travis, is also within Austin's city limits.

Cities of oil

Some cities in the Southwest grew for reasons other than a water supply. Oklahoma City and Tulsa existed before the discovery of oil, but the oil industry helped these two cities to grow. Oil was discovered in Tulsa in the early 1900s and in Oklahoma City 25 years later. Oklahoma is so oil-rich that there is actually oil under its capitol.

Dallas, Texas, became an important center for the oil industry, even though there has never been oil found in this part of Texas. Dallas grew because it was the center of the cotton trade and later grew into an oil center as well.

Ghost towns

Some towns in the Southwest started because of gold, copper, and silver mining. People would settle here as long as the **mines** were still going. However, when the mines were shut down, people left the towns. Today, there are more than 100 ghost towns in the Southwest.

The city of Dallas is an important center for the banking and energy businesses.

A walk through history

Much of the Southwest's history is contained in its cities. The Alamo, located in San Antonio, Texas, attracts thousands of visitors each year. In Dallas a reconstruction of the city's first cabin sits in a downtown park, while in Houston, you can visit the Johnson Space Center.

Santa Fe, New Mexico, is home to the Palace of the Governors, the oldest public building in the United States. Phoenix, Arizona, is home to the Pioneer Living History Museum, which traces 250 years of life in Arizona.

The displays at the Johnson Space Center in Houston, Texas include some of the original suits worn by the early astronauts. ▶

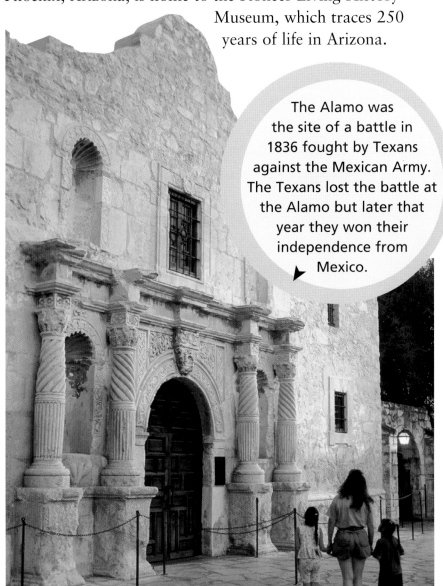

The Alamo was the site of a battle in 1836 fought by Texans against the Mexican Army. The Texans lost the battle at the Alamo but later that year they won their independence from ▶ Mexico.

National tragedies

Two great tragedies took place in the Southwest. On April 9, 1995, a terrorist's bomb exploded outside the Alfred P. Murrah Federal Building and took the lives of 168 people. The Oklahoma City National Memorial now stands in the building's place. Another sad event in American history took place on November 22, 1963, when President John F. Kennedy was shot and killed in Dallas. A memorial marks the site of that tragedy.

Southwestern towns

Southwestern towns each have a personality of their own. Nature is an important element in the lives of people living in towns such as Sedona, Arizona and Taos, New Mexico. Another town, the hill country community of Lockhart, Texas, is known for its antique auction and its barbecue restaurants.

Silver City, New Mexico, started as a mining town but was not deserted, thanks to its beautiful location and climate. Today it is a little treasure nestled in the hills near the Gila National Forest.

Was Roswell, New Mexico, the site of a UFO crash? Believers visit the town by the thousands every year.

Alien visitors

Roswell was the site of a mysterious crash in 1947. Something fell from the sky, but the military would not say what it was. Some claim to have seen alien passengers taken away! Today, the town draws **UFO** believers from all over the world.

Off the beaten path

Small town life is a big deal in Oklahoma. It is why many people love the state. At the turn of the century, Oklahoma was home to several "all-black" towns such as Boley, which became a town in 1905. From the late 1860s right into the early 1900s, all-black towns were built and governed by African Americans.

Here, people were free from racial **prejudice** and could follow their dreams in a supportive community. At the time, no towns like these existed anywhere else in the United States. The most famous of these towns was Boley, Oklahoma. Today, it includes people from a range of backgrounds.

The pueblo style of architecture is still in use today. Several families share this building in Taos, New Mexico. ⌄

Billy the Kid

William Henry McCarty, who was better known as Billy the Kid, lived in Silver City, New Mexico, as a boy in the 1860s. He was arrested at the age of 14, and later made the first of his many jailbreaks there. Billy the Kid became one of America's most famous outlaws. He lived on the run from his enemies and the law. In December 1880 the law caught up with Billy the Kid and he was captured. He escaped, but within a few years he was shot and killed by a sheriff in New Mexico.

Rural Life

Keeping the peace

With outlaws like Billy the Kid, Butch Cassidy, and Bonnie and Clyde roaming the old Southwest, the business of "keeping the peace" has always called for tough lawmen. From old-time sheriffs like the legendary Wyatt Earp to highly trained experts like the Texas Rangers, the region has always prided itself on keeping the bad guys at bay.

The cowboy is an important part of the rural history of the Southwest. The job of the cowboy was to round up the cattle after they had grazed, then drive them in one great herd to a place where they could be shipped by railroad to big cities.

As railroads moved closer to the cattle and as the great open spaces of the region were fenced in, the cattle drives ended and the ranching business grew. A ranch is a place where cattle live within fenced areas before being shipped to market. Once ranches were established, there was no longer a need for cowboys to round up cattle.

When the long cattle drives ended in the late 1800s, the region's cowboys turned to ranching. This job required different skills, but just as much toughness.

Cowboys today

Cowboys did not entirely disappear, but their jobs changed. In fact, thousands of cowboys work on the ranches of the Southwest to this day. Modern **technology** has replaced many of their traditional skills, but their talents are still on display at the rodeos held all around the region.

Rodeo competitions grew out of the contests cowboys made up to amuse themselves and pass the time. Rodeos are now one of the most popular sports in the Southwest.

This man is acting the part of a buffalo soldier. ➤

The popularity of the rodeo in the Southwest dates back to the early days of ranching, when cowboys would test their roping and riding skills against one another. ▼

At home with horses

Many of the cowboys who came to the Southwest in the 1860s and 1870s were freed slaves who were already experts at working with horses. Other freed slaves joined the U.S. Army and became "buffalo soldiers." This is an important part of the African-American history of the region, because many families in the Southwest can trace their families back to this time.

Ranching and farming

Rural life in the Southwest can be lonely and remote, but few who live out in the wide-open spaces would choose to move to the cities. Many who live far from crowded shopping malls and traffic jams make their living raising food or animals.

In Texas the two big crops are cotton and cattle—the two "C"s. The state is one of the world's leading producers of both. The rich soil deposited over thousands of years by the Rio Grande also makes Texas one of the nation's top producers of fruits and vegetables. **Aloe vera** products from the Rio Grande Valley are also important.

Grapefruit

Texas ruby reds are considered by many grapefruit-lovers to be the best-tasting grapefruit in the world. They grow only in the Rio Grande Valley in the rich farmland of Hidalgo County, near the Gulf of Mexico.

This Southwestern farmer and his two sons are out riding with their cattle.

What's growing?

Cattle has always been big business in Oklahoma. The state is also a major producer of wheat, hay, corn, soybeans, and peanuts. Oklahoma's eastern forests also keep the state's sawmills and paper producers busy.

In Arizona, more than 80 percent of the state's water supply is used for agriculture. Arizona's most important crop is cotton, but several different grains, as well as alfalfa, grow well in this part of the Southwest. Much of rural life in New Mexico centers around the cattle business.

Chili peppers

New Mexico is home to some of the world's most popular chili peppers. Farming can be very difficult in this dry climate, but hot peppers have thrived here for centuries. The kind of peppers grown here are called pungent peppers. New Mexico leads the nation in production of pungent peppers.

Cotton is an important crop in Arizona and throughout the Southwest.

33

Getting Around

With so much land to cover, the Southwest has always relied heavily on transportation. There were no horses in the Americas during ancient times, so people did not move unless they were following herds of game animals. When the Spanish came in the 1500s with their horses, carts, and cannons, they began constructing the first roads.

Railroads

The 1800s brought the railroad to the Southwest. The first rail link from the east to the west was completed in 1862, when tracks were laid between Santa Fe, New Mexico and San Diego, California. Railroads are still an important way to move products around the region.

The Royal Road

The first major road built in the Southwest went from Mexico City in Mexico to Santa Fe, New Mexico. It is called *El Camino Real*, or the Royal Road. It was built along an ancient trail used by the Pueblo people and later by Spanish colonists. *El Camino Real* runs for 13,000 miles (21,000 kilometers).

Trains like this one used to run on the Santa Fe Railroad. Today, modern trains have replaced old trains and new companies run the railways.

Transportation today

Today, most people get around the Southwest by car. Route 40 connects Oklahoma City and Albuquerque, while Route 10 connects Houston and Phoenix. Major north-south interstates include Route 25 and Route 35. Texas, with 77,000 miles (123,200 kilometers) of paved roadways, has the nation's largest highway system.

The Southwest plays an important role in air travel. Dallas-Fort Worth International, Houston's George Bush Intercontinental, and Phoenix Sky Harbor International all serve as bases for major airlines. Millions of international travelers reach their final destinations through these airports.

Saddle up!

One of the most popular means of transportation in the Southwest is also one of the oldest. Thousands of tourists take mule rides to the bottom of the Grand Canyon each year. These trips are not for everyone— the paths are steep and dangerous, temperatures often climb above 100 °F (38 °C), and riders can spend five or more very bumpy hours in the saddle.

Sky Harbor International Airport in Phoenix, Arizona is one of the busiest airports in the region.

Work in the Area

Woody Guthrie

The Southwest has seen times of great wealth and crushing poverty. During the Great Depression, Woodrow Wilson "Woody" Guthrie brought attention to the hardships in the region through folk songs. Guthrie was born in Okemah, Oklahoma in 1912, the same year that Woodrow Wilson was elected president. Woody Guthrie is perhaps best known for the folk song "This Land is Your Land."

A century ago, most of the workers in the Southwest made their livelihood from the earth. They raised crops and animals on it or used its **resources**. These industries still employ millions of people, but the region now has a much wider range of businesses.

Jobs in the Southwest

The Southwest has become a home for the technology and aerospace industries. The region has several major companies that make **microchips**, computers, and telecommunications products. This creates jobs for people of many different skills and education levels.

The Southwest has become an attractive place for technology companies to manufacture their products. ▼

Mexico

The Southwest shares a long border with Mexico, and many goods flow in and out of the United States through this part of the region. All of these products must be moved, stored, and sometimes assembled. For this reason, many people in the region have jobs related to cross-border businesses, including **manufacturing**, trucking, and warehousing.

The shared border with Mexico brings many people from the country looking for work in the Southwest. Many are migrant workers who move from place to place in order to find work. Most often the work they find is low-paying work on farms.

Workers pick strawberries on a Texas farm. Fruit grown in Texas ends up in stores all over the country.

The right stuff

The Southwest has inspired some of the world's finest architects, or people who design houses and buildings. Their challenge is to design homes and buildings that stand in harmony with nature. The most famous of these architects was Frank Lloyd Wright, who made Taliesin West in Scottsdale, Arizona his winter home and studio from 1937 to 1959.

From the ground up

The most important employer in the Southwest is the energy business. Trillions of dollars in oil, gas, coal, chemicals, and minerals are extracted from the earth and processed in this region each year. The work is hard and dirty, but it is necessary to fuel the United States.

Texas refineries have the important job of taking crude oil and gas pumped out of the ground and turning it into the gasoline people buy at service stations. Refined oil also helps machines run smoothly and is used as the gas with which millions of Americans heat their homes. Jobs in refineries are important to both the region—and the country as a whole.

Copper

More than half the copper produced in the United States comes from mines in Arizona. Copper is mined from large, open-pit and underground mines in the state. Copper is used to make everything from electrical wire to coins.

These men are drilling for oil in the Austin Chalk area of Texas.

Tourism

The Southwest's many cultures and fascinating history attract many visitors to the region. This has created great opportunities in the tourism industry. Texas is the third most visited state in the United States. The state brings in almost as many tourists as Florida and California. More than 25 million people visit Texas each year from outside the state.

Many young people get their first jobs in the tourism industry. Older workers are welcome in this industry, too. Their knowledge of history and their personal connections to the people, places, and things that make the Southwest special are important to tourism.

London Bridge...in Arizona!

Towns and cities compete for tourists, and some go to great lengths. Lake Havasu City in Arizona actually bought the old London Bridge, the same bridge in the famous children's song "London Bridge is Falling Down." They bought it in 1971, had it shipped from London, England, in pieces, and reassembled it when it arrived. It is one of Arizona's biggest attractions.

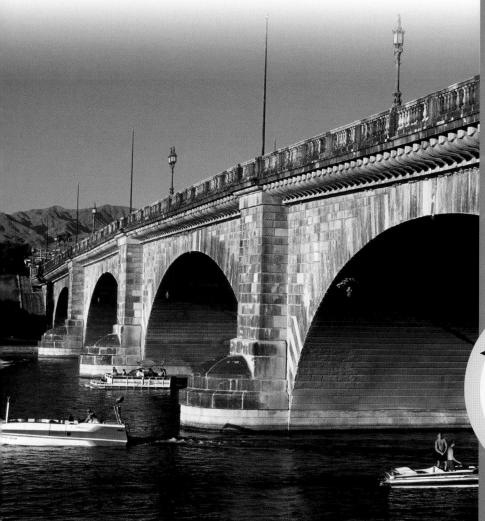

◄ Lake Havasu's reconstructed London Bridge is one of the region's most popular tourist attractions.

39

Free Time

Mariachis

One of the most popular forms of entertainment in the Southwest is mariachi music, a lively style of music that started in Spain. Mariachis dress in costumes and play at almost every Mexican festival. The best in the business come to Arizona for the International Mariachi Conference in Tucson and the Christmas Mariachi Concert in Phoenix.

For almost 200 years, Mexican, Native American, European, and other cultures have blended together in the Southwest. This has created forms of art, music, and food that can be found nowhere else in the world. It has also encouraged art forms that are true to each culture's roots.

In cities such as El Paso, located on the Texas-Mexico border, you can experience Mexican cooking, witness a Native American ceremonial dance, and listen to an old-time Texas swing band—all in the same day.

This mariachi band is performing in Tumacacori, Arizona, near the Mexican border.

Music

Music is an important part of the Southwest's culture. Fueled by experimental artists and people eager to hear new sounds, music has also become big business in the Southwest. One music center in the region is Austin. Music producers make regular trips to the Texas capital to look for new talent.

Museums

Everyone can enjoy the museums found in the Southwest. Houston's Museum of Fine Arts, its Contemporary Arts Museum, and the Dallas Museum of Art are among the best in the world. In Fort Worth, there is the Kimbell Art Museum and Museum of Modern Art. The Gilcrease Museum in Tulsa, Oklahoma, has one of the world's greatest collections of western art.

Cultural celebrations, such as parades featuring traditional Mexican dancing, are extremely popular in the Southwest. ▼

Native American art

To see one of the world's finest collections of Southwestern art, you have to leave the region's big cities and go to Taos, New Mexico. In the Millicent Rogers Museum are some of the finest examples of Apache baskets, Hopi art, and Navajo rugs, as well as a breathtaking collection of modern pottery.

41

Southwest cuisine

People in the Southwest are very serious about their food. The different cultures take great pride in their cooking. They also like to experiment by inventing cross-cultural specialties. The great quantity of fruits, vegetables, meats, and spices in this region means there are always plenty of fresh ingredients.

Some say you can guess which part of the Southwest you are in by "listening" to your tongue. In the northwestern sections, the food is influenced by Native American flavors. In the southern parts, people use a lot of Mexican spices. In central Texas and Oklahoma, barbecue is king.

Chili

Want to start an argument? Ask someone from the Southwest how to make chili. There are literally thousands of different recipes—and no one can agree on which one is the original or which one tastes the best.

Crawfish is a popular menu item at Gulf Coast restaurants.

A world of flavor

No city in the Southwest has more restaurants than Houston. Every style of cooking in the region can be found there. People from West Africa and Asia also offer traditional foods from many different countries and have begun to blend their cooking styles with local ones.

The region's most interesting food can be found in New Mexico, where cooking is considered an art form—the same as painting and sculpture. Starting with the basics of corn, beans, and chili peppers, the chefs in this area create traditional country dishes or blend them with other styles of cooking.

New Mexico farms produce some of the world's best chili peppers.

A celebration in Phoenix would not be complete without a helping of *carne asada*, grilled steak served Mexican style.

Red or green?

When you sit down for a meal in many restaurants in the Southwest, one of the biggest decisions you will have to make is "red or green?" The question is whether you prefer red chili sauce or green chili sauce. Green chilis can be very spicy. Red can be more flavorful.

43

Sports in the Southwest

Because cities in this region are so far apart, **professional** (pro) sports teams often have fans who live far away. These fans usually divide their loyalty between the closest pro team and the team from a local high school or college. Before professional sports came to the Southwest, high-school and college football were number one. In many areas, they still are.

The first city in the Southwest to have a successful professional sports team was Dallas. In 1960 the Cowboys of the National Football League played their first season. Today there are also pro football teams in Phoenix and Houston.

SPORT KINGS GUM

JIM THORPE

Jim Thorpe, born in Oklahoma, is still regarded as the country's greatest all-around athlete.

The Dallas Cowboys are a popular NFL team in the Southwest.

Jim Thorpe

Jim Thorpe, a Native American, was born on the Sac and Fox reservation in Oklahoma in 1887. He was a football, baseball, basketball, and track star in the early 1900s. Thorpe won two gold medals at the 1912 Olympics.

Baseball and basketball

In 1962 baseball's Houston Colt .45s joined the National League. They became the Astros in 1965, when they moved into the AstroDome. Today there are also pro baseball teams in Phoenix and Dallas–Fort Worth.

Pro basketball came to the Southwest later in the 1960s. The Dallas Chaparrals played their first season in 1967. They became the San Antonio Spurs in 1973. The Phoenix Suns began to play in 1968. Today there are also basketball teams in Houston and Dallas.

SPORT KINGS GUM

"BABE" DIDRICKSON

"Babe" Didrikson, born in Texas, made headlines as a track star in the 1930s and was the greatest female golfer of the 1940s.

Babe Didrikson

Mildred "Babe" Didrikson was born in Port Arthur, Texas, in 1914. She was a champion basketball and baseball player, top-ranked golfer, and Olympic gold medalist in track and field. Didrikson once defeated the entire University of Illinois track squad in a team meet—by herself!

The Phoenix Suns score points against the Dallas Mavericks in this NBA playoff game.

45

White out!

One of the coolest things to do in New Mexico is dune surfing at White Sands National Monument. All you need is a good snowboard and a little practice to glide down the dunes, which are made of white sand washed down from the San Andreas and Sacramento Mountains.

Taking time out

How do people relax in the Southwest? They head for open spaces. The different types of land and climates in the region offer many choices. From hiking to fishing, swimming, boating, or skiing, there is something for everyone in the Southwest.

When the weather is hot, many people look for ways to cool off in the water. The region's many dams, built to provide water for drinking and **irrigation,** also created large lakes. Two-thirds of the lakes in Oklahoma, for example, are made in this way. These lakes, and the rivers they feed, are great places for people who love water sports.

New Mexico's Sandia Peak offers extreme bikers extreme views of the valley below. Mountain biking is one of the region's most popular sports.

The great outdoors

Sport fishing is another favorite leisure activity for the people of the Southwest. The lakes and rivers of the region are full of aquatic life, while the Gulf of Mexico is home to some of the best deep-water fishing in the world.

You will probably have to bring your own water when you visit the deserts of New Mexico and Arizona. Still, there are few places on earth where a person feels closer to nature. The desert can be challenging, but the scenery is worth the effort. The views are even better from the mountains, where everyone from day hikers to experienced climbers can find a trail to their liking. Skiers and snowboarders enjoy the fresh powder on the peaks between Taos and Santa Fe in New Mexico.

Snow day

Although many people think of dry, hot desert when they think of the Southwest, skiers and snowboarders know better. They enjoy the fresh powder on many peaks throughout the region.

One of the most popular activities in Arizona is a rafting trip down the Colorado River.

Rodeos

Rodeos are not just sporting events. They also celebrate the culture of the Southwest. Horse shows and rodeos are therefore very popular in the region. The biggest event of the year is Oklahoma's International Finals Rodeo—the "Super Bowl" of the rodeo world. Another favorite is *La Fiesta de los Vaqueros,* which means Celebration of the Cowboys in Arizona.

Festivals, fairs, and holidays

Rarely a week goes by without a major fair or festival in the Southwest. People from different cultures gather in cities and towns all across the region to celebrate. From the Native American Waila Festival in Tucson, Arizona, to the Shakespeare Festival in Odessa, Texas, there is something for everyone.

The biggest celebrations in the region take place around *Cinco de Mayo,* which is Spanish for Fifth of May. It was on that day in 1862 when the Mexicans defended their country in a victory over the French. September 16th, the anniversary of Mexican independence, is another time of great celebration.

The annual rodeo in Payson, Arizona has been held every year since 1884.

History—ancient and recent

Native American festivals can be found in New Mexico. They often take place at ancient pueblos and feature bright ceremonial costumes that are only displayed on special occasions.

Another popular gathering in the region is the Route 66 Festival in Albuquerque, New Mexico. For more than 50 years, Route 66 was how most Americans got their first look at the Southwest. The road snaked its way from Chicago, Illinois to the Pacific Ocean—more than 2,400 miles (3,840 kilometers). Route 66 was broken up in 1985 and is no longer used by long-distance travelers.

Owners of classic cars often drive on sections of the old Route 66.

An Amazing Region

Great artists

The Southwest has inspired many great artists, including Frederic Remington (1861–1909) and Georgia O'Keeffe (1887–1986). Remington's paintings and sculptures brought the region to life for Americans. O'Keeffe's paintings of the New Mexican deserts and its flowers gave art lovers a personal connection to the region's beauty.

Warm weather, cloudless skies, modern highways, good food, and great people—it is no wonder that many Americans move to the Southwest every year. These people further add to the mix of a culturally diverse people that grew out of the Southwest's rich history of Native Americans, Spanish colonies, and American settlers.

The spirit of the Southwest has its roots in cultures that date back centuries. As different groups came into the region, each added something new to the culture of the Southwest.

Horseriding skills were not limited to the men in the Southwest's early days, nor are they today. Women's events are among the most popular at the region's rodeos.

Southwestern spaces

The climate and land in the Southwest also give the region a certain flavor. Hot, dry deserts, deep, wide canyons, and wide open spaces help to define life in the Southwest. Pastimes in the region include rodeos and festivals that celebrate the history and culture of the region's people.

In this book, you have learned how the four states that make up this region share many qualities. You have also learned how each state differs from the others.

Great writers

The Southwest has produced many great writers, including Ralph Ellison (1913–1994), who was born in Oklahoma City. His 1952 novel *Invisible Man* described racial problems in America from the African-American point of view.

Hopi dancers perform a traditional dance in Mesa Verde, New Mexico.

Find Out More

World Wide Web

The Fifty States
www.infoplease.com/states.html

This website has a clickable U.S. map that gives facts about each of the 50 states, plus images of each state's flag.

These sites have pictures, statistics, and other facts about each state in the Southwest region:

Arizona
www.az.gov

New Mexico
www.state.nm.uk

Oklahoma
www.ok.gov

Texas Senate Kids
www.senate.state.tx.us/kids/

Books to read

Ciovacco, Justine, Kathleen A. Feeley, and Kristen Behrens. *State-By-State Atlas*. New York: DK Publishing, 2003.

Fifer, Barbara. *Everyday Geography of the United States*. Black Dog & Leventhal, 2000.

Strudwick, Leslie. *Oklahoma*. Mankato, Minn.: Weigl Publishers, 2001.

Places to visit

The Alamo (San Antonio, Texas)
Barton Springs Pool (Austin, Texas)
Carlsbad Caverns National Park (New Mexico)
Dallas Museum of Art Dallas (Texas)
Gilcrease Museum Tulsa (Oklahoma)
Kimbell Art Museum Fort Worth (Texas)
Monument Valley State Park (Arizona and Utah)
Museum of Fine Arts Houston (Texas)
Myriad Botanical Gardents Oklahoma City (Oklahoma)

Timeline

15,000 BC
Nomadic groups begin to hunt big game in the region.

9500
The Clovis people are thought to settle in the Southwest.

1000
The first settlements begin along the Rio Grande River, with people living in pit houses.

AD 300
People living in the Southwest start farming in the region.

1540
Spanish explorers arrive in the Southwest.

1595
First Spanish colony is established near Santa Fe.

1610
Sante Fe, the second-oldest city in the United States, is founded.

1862
The first railway linking the eastern and western United States is completed.

1848
The United States seizes New Mexico and Arizona.

1846
The United States and Mexico go to war.

1845
Texas becomes the 28th state.

1836
Texas rises up against the Mexican government and wins independence from Mexico.

1821
Mexico declares independence from Spain.

1821
Santa Fe Trail is established.

1803
United States buys Oklahoma from France as part of the Louisiana Purchase.

1900
The port city of Galveston, Texas is destroyed by a hurricane.

1907
Oklahoma becomes the 46th state.

1911
The Roosevelt Dam is built on the Salt River to provide water to Phoenix and surrounding areas.

1912
New Mexico and Arizona become the 47th and 48th states.

1930s
Thousands of families leave the Southwest after having their homes and farms destroyed by the Dust Bowl.

1952
Texan Dwight Eisenhower is elected the 34th president of the United States.

1963
President John F. Kennedy is assassinated in Dallas, Texas; Texan Lyndon Johnson becomes president of the United States.

2005
Hurricane Rita smashes into the east coast of Texas.

2001
The Arizona Diamondbacks become the first Southwest baseball team to win the World Series.

2000
Texas governor George W. Bush is elected president of the United States.

1995
The Murrah Federal Building in Oklahoma City is destroyed by a terrorist's bomb.

1964
Johnson is elected president in a landslide victory.

States at a Glance

Arizona

Nickname: The Grand Canyon State
Became State: 1912
Capital: Phoenix
Motto: *Ditat Deus*—God enriches
Flower: Saguaro blossom
Tree: Paloverde
Animal: Ringtail
Bird: Cactus wren
Song: "Arizona"

New Mexico

Nickname: The Land of Enchantment
Became State: 1912
Capital: Santa Fe
Motto: *Crescit eundo*— It grows as it goes
Flower: Yucca
Tree: Pinon
Animal: Black bear
Bird: Roadrunner
Song: "O, Fair New Mexico"

Oklahoma

Nickname: The Sooner State
Became State: 1907
Capital: Oklahoma City
Motto: *Labor omnia vincit*— Labor conquers all things
Flower: Mistletoe
Tree: Redbud
Animal: Bison
Bird: Scissor-tailed flycatcher
Song: "Oklahoma!"

Texas

Nickname: The Lone Star State
Became State: 1845
Capital: Austin
Motto: Friendship
Flower: Bluebonnet
Tree: Pecan
Animals: Longhorn, armadillo, Mexican free-tailed bat
Bird: Mockingbird
Song: "Texas, Our Texas"

Glossary

aloe vera succulent plant used for lotions and other products

ancestors people from whom one is descended

aquifer layer of rock that contains vast amounts of water

archaeologists people who study past human life

bison large animal with shaggy head also called the North American buffalo

campus grounds of a school

canyon narrow valley with high, steep sides

climate weather conditions of a place

coastal plain flat, sandy land with few trees, located near an ocean or gulf

cultures customs, language, art, and ideas shared by groups of people

deserts dry lands with few plants

economy system of money in a place

high plains elevated region of the Great Plains that lie east of the Rocky Mountains across much of the United States

irrigation supplying land with water

Louisiana Purchase agreement signed in 1803 in which the United States bought France's land in North America

manufacturing turning something into a useful product

microchips small chips that hold electronic information

mines places from which minerals (such as gold, silver, and coal) are taken

mesas steep hills with flat tops

nomadic having no fixed home; moving from place to place

pastimes activities that help pass the time

petrified turned to stone over millions of years

plateau high, flat area of land

prejudice opinion that is formed unfairly

professional performs a job for pay

pueblos large stone and adobe structure shared by a Native American community

republic nation ruled by representatives elected by the people

resources things that help people live

species group of animals or plants that are of the same type

technology the use of science to solve problems

tradition way of doing things that is passed from one generation to the next

tributary stream or river that flows into a larger river

UFO unidentified flying object

Index